The Publishers gratefully acknowledge assistance provided by Sir Knelson Wriddle, Gentleman Park-Keeper of the Realm, in compiling this book.

Publishers: Ladybird Books Ltd., Loughborough
Printed in England. If wet, Italy.

'How it works'

THE
DOG

by J.A. HAZELEY, N.S.F.W.
and J.P. MORRIS, O.M.G.

(Authors of 'Cooking Your Cat')

A LADYBIRD BOOK FOR GROWN–UPS

The dog is often called man's best friend.

Dogs are reliable, loyal and loving, like all best friends.

They also smell like a bobble hat full of corned beef that has been left on the parcel shelf of a locked car for a fortnight during a hot spell. But there are some things you don't mention to a best friend.

Some people say dogs can start to resemble their owners.

Thin people have thin dogs. Happy people have happy dogs.

This dog's owner is an award–winning Viennese rapper–cum–architect who collects antique surgical equipment and likes to put flowers in his salads.

Dogs can be trained as special helpers for people with many sorts of conditions.

Toto is training to be an asthma dog for people allergic to dog hair.

Tomorrow, she is being varnished and sealed before meeting her new owner.

Maisie and Joey are in the garden.

Everyone watches while Joey runs in energetic circles. They cannot understand what he is doing.

Joey is chasing air round the garden, of course.

Siobhán only buys Columbo the best food. It is grain—free, single—protein, holistic, hypo—allergenic and certified organic.

"You love it, don't you, boy?" says Siobhán.

Columbo does love the food. But he would be just as happy to eat his own sick.

Dog and man have been friends for many thousands of years.

Dognald is going to bury his owner's dinner in the garden, in case any hyenas or jackals or sabre-toothed tigers come and try to steal it.

Oscar knows that if he pops his head up on one side of a human's chair, he will get a little bit of what the human is eating.

Then if he pops his head up on the other side of her chair, he will count as a different dog, who has not had any food yet.

Dogs are cleverer than humans, thinks Oscar.

"Catch the ball, Moptop!" says Richard.

Richard does not throw the ball.

Moptop runs for a few yards then comes back for more, wagging his tail.

Richard wishes anything else he did in his life could make anyone as happy as not throwing a ball makes Moptop.

Lyttelton is confused.

There are two non—dogs in his bedroom.

Now his bedroom will smell of the non—dogs.

Lyttelton will have to make his bedroom smell nice again by weeing all over it.

Pippin loves her new toy. She chews it and chews it.

And chews it and chews it and chews it and chews it.

And chews it and chews it and chews it — and chews it and chews it and chews it and chews it. And chews it.

She will lose all interest once she finds out there is no meat inside.

George Harrison, one of The Beatles, was a devout Hindu.

Hindus believe in reincarnation — that they will come back to life in another form.

This might be George Harrison.

If so, George Harrison likes the ball.

Lorna comes home and finds that Muffin has had a little accident in the kitchen. She shouts at him and rubs his nose in it.

Muffin wonders what has upset Lorna. He decides it was the noise the front door made just now when Lorna came in.

Muffin goes and scratches the door to teach it a lesson, but Lorna shouts at him again.

Poor Muffin can get nothing right.

Steve's wife says he should walk rather than get the bus.

"I don't need to," says Steve. "I did 11,000 steps with Barney in the park this morning."

Steve doesn't mention that he attached his Fitbit to Barney's collar while he slumped on a bench with a Cumberland sausage bap.

So far this week, Jenna's dog Trubshaw has eaten a sweat sock, a pair of in—ear headphones, the contents of the brown recycling bin and an aromatherapy candle.

"Good boy, Trubshaw," says Jenna when he drops a hat at her feet without eating it.

Jenna hopes this does not mean Trubshaw has eaten a cub scout.

Once a week, Patsy vacuums up all the dog hair in her house.

When she has finished the sofa, she will do the carpets, inside the oven, in the powder tray of the washing machine, between the pages of the book she is reading, and behind the wallpaper.

"How did it get there?" laughs Patsy, coughing up a hair—ball.

Dogs do many jobs for man. They have been trained to hunt, guard, retrieve, track and herd.

Biggins has been trained not to bark while Vince steals a lamb, and not to eat the lamb until Vince has casseroled it.

Ali and Jo's "babies" are called Bubble and Squeak. They have booties, jumpers and bow ties, and at their joint birthday party, they both wore tiaras.

Ali and Jo go to church every Sunday, because they hope to get Bubble and Squeak into a Catholic obedience school.

Marlborough Perignon Kerwhizz is a pedigree dog. She is the highly—prized result of many years of careful in—breeding.

Her owners, the Duke and Duchess of Beaumarch, are the result of a similar process.

The first animal to orbit the earth was a dog called Laika.

Dogs are good at orbiting, as long as they have been trained not to stick their heads out of the window.

Dogs change over time.

In the 16th century, this Prussian Tinhound's shiny coat was highly prized and the animal was bred to exaggerate it.

A modern Tinhound played the part of K9 in Doctor Who.

John is dog—sitting. Pickles keeps barking at the fridge.

"It can't be these sausages," thinks John, "because there is a dog called a sausage. And a sausage called a hot dog. Dogs are not cannibals."

John gets Pickles a lovely plate of butter.

Pickles cannot wait for John's sister to get out of hospital. John is not really a dog person.

Benji has found something.

"It looks like a spiky mouse," thinks Benji. "I bet it is good to play with."

It is not good for Benji or for Benji's owner. But it is good for the vet, whose bill is over £400.

Dora's big dog Pugwash has frightened a little girl in the park.

"Pugwash would not frighten anyone," says Dora.

"The little girl was frightened," says the policeman.

"Well, he never frightens me," says Dora.

The policeman can see in Dora's eyes that the case is closed.

Beano dreams he has been invited to a party to celebrate the defeat of the human oppressor.

"Those fools," laughs the cat in charge. "How did they not guess we had been planning their overthrow for tens of thousands of years? Why did they think we agreed to live in their awful, hot homes?"

Beano doesn't understand the politics, but he is delighted to be allowed up on the furniture.

THE AUTHORS would like to record their gratitude and offer their apologies to the many Ladybird artists whose luminous work formed the glorious wallpaper of countless childhoods. Revisiting it for this book as grown-ups has been a privilege.

MICHAEL JOSEPH

UK | USA | Canada | Ireland | Australia
India | New Zealand | South Africa

Michael Joseph is part of the Penguin Random House group of companies
whose addresses can be found at global.penguinrandomhouse.com

First published 2016
001

Copyright © Jason Hazeley and Joel Morris, 2016
All images copyright © Ladybird Books Ltd, 2016

The moral right of the authors has been asserted

Printed in Italy by L.E.G.O. S.p.A

A CIP catalogue record for this book is available from the British Library

ISBN: 978–0–718–18435–3

www.greenpenguin.co.uk

MIX
Paper from
responsible sources
FSC® C018179

Penguin Random House is committed to a
sustainable future for our business, our readers
and our planet. This book is made from Forest
Stewardship Council® certified paper.